The HEART of ADDICTION

Workbook

MARK E. SHAW

The Heart of Addiction Workbook
by Mark Shaw

Copyright 2008 © FOCUS PUBLISHING, INC.
All rights reserved.

No part of this book may be reproduced by any means
without written consent of the publisher
except for brief quotes used in reviews written specifically
for use in a magazine or newspaper.

Scripture references are quoted from
The English Standard Version of the Bible
and where noted,
The King James Version
and The New King James Version

Cover design by Melanie Schmidt

ISBN 1-885904-69-X
978-1-885904-69-0

PRINTED IN THE UNITED STATES OF AMERICA
BY
FOCUS PUBLISHING
Bemidji, Minnesota

Why a Workbook?

One of the "untapped" resources for overcoming a substance abuse problem or any type of "addiction" is the Bible. God's Word has much to say concerning the problem of "addiction" though His Word uses different terminology for good reasons. One of the primary purposes of this workbook is to teach you what God's Word says about "addiction." My goal is to help you to develop a biblical perspective so that you can effectively overcome your "addiction."

A second purpose of this workbook is for you as an individual to grow closer to God by completing these assignments in your private, devotional time with your Creator: the Lord Jesus Christ. God is relational and created you to have a thriving relationship with Him. He also wants to use your life to reflect Himself and His glory to a lost and dying world.

As someone who has struggled with a life-devastating sin like "addiction," you likely have not been functioning effectively in God's plan for your life. Since the Holy Spirit illuminates God's will, character, love, plan, and purpose for your life, you can learn how to become more obedient to God and more Christ-like in your thoughts, words, and actions in overcoming this serious problem of substance abuse. In so doing, you will reap blessings in this life and in the eternal life to come. I Timothy 4:7-8: "**Have nothing to do with irreverent, silly myths. Rather _train yourself_ for godliness; for while bodily training is of some value, godliness is of value in every way, as it holds promise for the present life and also for the life to come**"[1] (emphasis mine).

The third important purpose of the workbook is that you cultivate a real, intimate relationship with another human being. You will notice that many of the assignments ask you to share your answers with a **T**rusted **C**hristian **F**riend (TCF). If you complete the answers to the workbook but fail to share those answers with a TCF, then you will not receive the maximum benefits from this workbook which is intended to gently push you to become more relational with others. The process of overcoming your "addiction" starts with discipleship in at least one meaningful, intimate relationship with a mentor, friend, or biblical counselor.

As you know, you cannot overcome your addiction alone in your own strength. You need the power of the Holy Spirit as well as the support, nurture, love, encouragement, and admonition of people who care about you. For this reason, plan to share your answers with others: your pastor, mentor, church leaders, accountability partners, trusted Christian friend (**TCF**), or biblical counselor. Ask these persons to read Appendix I in The Heart of Addiction book if they are concerned about how best to help you.

If you are currently living in a residential program with others who struggle with similar addictive problems, then share your answers with group members AFTER each person has had an opportunity to answer the questions by spending time alone with the Lord. Small groups led by a mature, committed Christian can be an excellent resource for your growth in Christ. Ideally, if you are dealing with any form of "idolatry" and physical "addiction," then it is highly recommended that you meet with a certified biblical counselor to deal with your spiritual and emotional issues as well as a primary physician to address your physical issues.

---

[1] Unless otherwise noted, all Scripture references have been excerpted from *The Holy Bible: English standard version.* 2001 (electronic ed.). Good News Publishers: Wheaton.

The best way to know God and how He has designed you for His purposes is to study the Bible; therefore, this workbook is intended to be a helpful tool for you to use as you study your Bible and the text, <u>The Heart of Addiction</u>. You will be challenged to go deeper into the Word of God. Like any tool, however, you must use it to the best of your ability in order for it to do its job. No one buys a hammer and says to the tool, "Hammer, do your thing while I sit over here and watch television!" That is ridiculous but many of us expect to buy a workbook without doing the work required in order to benefit the most from it. Don't be that person; instead, take the advice that Paul encouraged Timothy with in 2 Timothy 2:15: **"Do your best to present yourself to God as one approved, a worker who has no need to be ashamed, rightly handling the word of truth."**

If you are *not* a Christian, continue to read the book, workbook, and especially Appendix B. You need the Holy Spirit's power to help you overcome your "addiction." You may be surprised at how superior God's wisdom is when compared to the world's knowledge.

If you are already a Christian, you will be challenged and encouraged as you work at growing spiritually. The three themes you will notice resounding in this workbook are:

1. Who are you (the substance abuser, "addict," idolater, or "alcoholic")?
2. What are alcohol, drugs, and substances and how are they to be used to serve God?
3. Who is God and how do we know Him and serve Him?

My prayer for you is from Hebrews 13:20-21:

> **"Now may the God of peace who brought again from the dead our Lord Jesus, the great shepherd of the sheep, by the blood of the eternal covenant, equip you with everything good that you may do his will, working in us that which is pleasing in his sight, through Jesus Christ, to whom be glory forever and ever. Amen."**

How To Make The Most Of This Workbook

Instructions

1. It is strongly recommended that you read each chapter of <u>The Heart of Addiction</u> book prior to working in your workbook. It is best to read through the chapter once. Then, open your workbook and answer the questions referring back to the corresponding chapter. You will need the book to answer some of the questions in the workbook.

2. Throughout this workbook, you will notice squares like this: ☐

Check each box when you have completed the assigned task. Put the date of completion in the box or beside the box.

3. There are blank lines provided for you to use in answering the questions and writing out your thoughts, feelings, and behaviors. Some of the lines simply ask a "yes" or "no" question. Fill out your answers completely and write more in the margins or in your personal journal. Be honest because the Lord already knows what is in your heart.

4. You are strongly encouraged to buy an inexpensive, spiral notebook, which will serve as your personal journal in which to write your prayers, confessions of sin, plans of repentance, thoughts, feelings, actions, successes, failures, lessons learned, and more. You will be glad that you recorded your thoughts, feelings, and behaviors in a journal one day in the future when you are able to reflect upon what the Lord has completed through you and how He has grown you into spiritual maturity.

5. Dive in and study the Bible deeply. The Lord is infinite and knows an infinite number of things. He cannot reveal it all to you because you do not have the capacity to understand and contain it all; however, He wants you to know more about Him and His character than you know right now. He desires for you to know Him intimately as your Father, King, Creator, and Friend. Spend time with God in a real and vibrant relationship just as you would a friend on earth. Prayer is talking to God; Bible study is listening to God as He speaks through His revealed Word of Truth to you. Use this workbook as an opportunity to grow closer to the Lord and to a trusted Christian friend (TCF).

MESSAGE to TCF: Although it is implied by your title, "Trusted Christian Friend", we want to be certain that you understand and take the position seriously. As you work through this workbook with your friend, you will notice that he or she is encouraged to discuss their ideas and challenges with you. It is important that you not betray their trust by discussing their progress with anyone else without their permission.

Table of Contents

Why a Workbook?
How to Make the Most of this Workbook
Introduction

Section 1: Teaching	**Page**
1. A Spiritual Problem	7
2. Man's Theories and God's Truth	14
3. Redefining the World's Terminology	21
4. Who Are You?	24
5. Frequently Asked Questions	27
6. The Good Purpose of Drugs and Alcohol	31
7. Drunkenness	33
8. The Depiction of Substance Abuse from Proverbs 23	41
9. The Physical Components of Addiction	43
10. Idolatry	44
11. The Perishing Mentality	47
12. Heart Problems	51
Section 2: Reproof	
13. How Many Enemies Do You Have?	54
14. The Spiritual Consequences of Addiction	57
15. Manifestations of Pride	59
16. What to do First: Put-Off	61
Section 3: Correction	
17. What to do Second: Renewing Your Mind	63
18. The Battle in the Mind	66
Section 4: Training in Righteousness	
19. What to do Third: Put-On	69
20. Responsibility, Gratitude, and Submission: More to Put-On	71
21. Seven Things for Which to Pray	75
22. Taking a Nazirite Vow under the Care of a Physician	77
23. Controlled by the Holy Spirit	79
24. Focusing Upon Others	82
25. The End of the Matter is Just the Beginning	85
Additional Bible Study on "Drunkenness"	87

Introduction

1. Read the Introduction of *The Heart of Addiction*.

2. Read Appendix K in the text, which is entitled "Words of Instruction and Caution."

3. Read 2 Timothy 3:16-17: "All Scripture is breathed out by God and profitable for teaching, for reproof, for correction, and for training in righteousness that the man of God may be competent, equipped for every good work."

In the blank that follows, write your answer to the following question:
Where does your power to change come from? _____

If you answered anything other than the Lord Jesus Christ, then your answer is incorrect. The transforming power and hope that is offered to you is in Christ Jesus alone. There is no such thing as an individual having "will power" apart from Christ, but there is the "will of God power" available to all Christians by the indwelling of the Holy Spirit.

Here are the three requirements that you must meet in order to experience lasting change:

1) First, you must be a **Christian.** In 2 Timothy 3:16 above, the Bible is speaking to the "man of God" which is a person who has been born again.
Are you a Christian? _____

If you answered "yes," then write out your testimony of how you came to personally know Christ in your journal. Share this testimony with a friend by reading it to them soon.

If you answered "no" then read Appendix B immediately.

2) Second, you must believe in the **supremacy of Scripture**, the **Holy Bible**. When you believe in the supremacy of Scripture, it means that you are agreeing that God's Word is authoritative and to be obeyed when rightly interpreted. God's Word is the final and absolute authority when interpreted correctly.

Do you believe in the supremacy of Scripture and are you committed to being a hearer and a doer of God's Word? _____

3) Third, you must believe that work is required in the life of a believer. You are not working your way toward heaven, but you are working so that the Holy Spirit can transform your character on a daily basis by becoming more and more obedient to Christ. The work that you do is only accomplished through the power of the Holy Spirit according to **Philippians 2:12-13**: "**Therefore, my beloved, as you have always obeyed, so now, not only as in my presence but much more in my absence, work out your own salvation with fear and trembling, for it is God who works in you, both to will and to work for his good pleasure.**" This partnership of the Holy Spirit working inside of you is called sanctification and it is a lifelong process of grace.

A word of warning about your partnership with the Holy Spirit is that it is possible for a Christian to **"quench the Holy Spirit"** according to **I Thessalonians 5:19**. This means that Christians can live to fulfill the selfish desires of their flesh rather than to fulfill the divine desires of the Lord.

Do you believe that the Holy Spirit works inside you to produce what God desires for you? _____

(Write your answer and <u>speak</u> it to your friend. Please do not skip the confessional part of speaking your belief aloud to a friend because it is very important!)

4. *Are you willing to dispose of the world's definitions of your problems and embrace what God says about your life?*

Using the non-biblical terms "substance abuser" and "addict" and "alcoholic" suggests that one is less responsible before God and that is not true. The substance abuser and addict are responsible before God for the thoughts, words, and behaviors that led to becoming physically addicted to alcohol and drugs. Christians are capable of being physically addicted to a drug; therefore, the words "substance abuser" and "addict" will be utilized in this book with caution, and with the understanding that God's answers for addiction are spiritual, powerful, practical, and hopeful for believers. Be conformed to God's ways and transformed by the renewing of your mind. Do not attempt to make God's ways conform to your desires. God is your sovereign, infinitely wise Creator.

So I ask you, are you willing to dispose of the world's terminologies and see your life through God's eyes? Circle your answer.

YES   NO

One more concept to begin contemplating is "sin." Read Genesis chapters 1-3 to understand that God created a good and perfect world that mankind's sinful disobedience ruined. The word "good" biblically does not fall in the sequence of "good, better, best" as is often implied in our English language. The word "good" has a biblical meaning of something as "perfect" with *nothing bad in it*. When we say that God is good, we mean He alone has nothing bad in Him. He is perfect. Mankind, however, became corrupt after The Fall in Genesis 3 as each person since that day has been born with what we call a "sin nature." The Bible says that no one does good in Romans 3:12 meaning that we all have some "bad" in us called sin. Sin lives within our nature but we learn to say "no" to sin and to say "yes" to the Holy Spirit as born again Christians. In Christ, we have the power to say "no" to sin.

A final note is that God labels "addiction" as sin since He holds us responsible for the sinful choices we make. God calls "addiction" two names in the Bible: "idolatry" is the general term and "drunkenness" is the specific term.[2] If you want a third label for it, according to Ephesians 5:18, "drunkenness" is "sin" as it reads: **"And do not get drunk with wine, for that is debauchery, but be filled with the Spirit."** As you study further, you will become more familiar with these biblical terms.

5. Assess your current state of chemical usage by circling the one that best applies to you:

1) I am an occasional yet excessive alcohol and drug abuser but I do NOT consider myself to be "addicted" physically
2) I am physically "addicted" to alcohol and drugs
3) I am in some other group. (Describe your group in the space below.)

_____

Be sure to share the answers to your self-assessment of recent chemical usage with a trusted Christian friend or biblical counselor.

6. What is your heart's primary desire when you drink alcohol or use drugs excessively? (circle all that apply below)

Avoid pain

Seek pleasure

Both

To the best of your ability, explain how this desire to please your physical body impacts your spiritual life: _____

---

[2] "Witchcraft," or *pharmakia*, is another term the Bible uses to describe addiction. *Pharmakia* is the Greek word related to our English word: pharmacy.

7. Ask for prayer support from others while you read this book.

Is there someone in your life right now (a Christian friend, pastor, family member, spouse, or loved one) who can commit to praying for you while you read and work through the concepts and instructions in this book? It may even be the person who gave you this book. Tell the person you have chosen that you are reading this book and ask them to commit to praying for you daily until you finish it. This may be a commitment for a few months or for a much longer period of time, so choose wisely whom you will ask. In the space provided here, write down the name and contact information of 3 possible candidates whom you could ask to pray for you during your study of this book. Contact them as soon as possible to get a firm commitment of support for you in prayer. You may be surprised to learn how willing other Christians are to pray for you.

List candidate(s) here:

_____
_____
_____

8. Ask someone to read this book with you.

Is there someone in your life right now (a Christian friend, pastor, family member, spouse, or loved one) who can commit to walking with you through this period of time in your life as you seek God's answers for your addiction? This may or may not be the same person described above. Actually, it is often better to get a different person so you can have more people resources to turn to for help.

You may need more than one person to fulfill this responsibility because the commitment level required for this task will be even greater than that of being a prayer partner. This person needs to have a deep love for God, be a strong, growing Christian person, and be willing to walk with you through this struggle. This person must be committed to making time for you in his/her schedule and willing to let you call them 24 hours a day if necessary. However, be respectful of their time, family commitments and sleep hours when possible.

Prayerfully find this person before you go any further. You cannot isolate. You cannot do this alone. You need God and his mighty resources. From this point on, we will refer to this person as your "TCF" which stands for "Trusted Christian Friend." Everyone needs a "TCF" – a **T**rusted **C**hristian **F**riend. Ask your TCF to read Appendix I to help him/her in the mentoring relationship. This person will be making what may be a short-lived, but intense, commitment to you for the duration of your study; however, this could turn into a lifelong relationship. Remember, in this book, we will be referring to this person throughout the rest of our study as your "TCF." List candidate(s) here:

_____
_____
_____

If you are unable to find a committed TCF, then keep working in the workbook. Pray each day asking God to send you a TCF. Keep your eyes open for the person(s) whom the Lord will send your way.

9. It would be extremely helpful for you to have a Bible on hand. Do you have a Bible? _____ If not, ask your TCF to help you to get one.

Read Appendix G in The Heart of Addiction book to help you to study the Bible effectively.

10. Your primary goal for changing your ways must be to please God and glorify Him in all your thoughts, words, and behaviors – not just to sober up and get your circumstances fixed. Have your circumstances (you might be in jail or in treatment now) driven you to now look for help? _____

If you do NOT think your primary goal right now is to please God, know that, by the grace of God, your study in this workbook can ultimately bring you to the place where life means this: fearing God and honoring Him by keeping His commandments.

If this is not a current desire of your heart, keep reading and praying that God, through the Holy Spirit and His Word, will change your heart's desires.

11. Are you currently active in a Christ-centered, Bible teaching church?
_____

If not, talk to your TCF about possible churches that you can "plug in" to OR begin to attend church with your TCF. Write down the name of the church you are going to faithfully attend:

_____

If you <u>are</u> a member of a church, then you already have relationships established to help you. You should humble yourself and ask your pastor for help, as well. Ask your pastor to commit to spending a little time with you each month in a discipleship relationship. If he cannot, then ask him to help you find a mature, same-gender church member (preferably a leader in the church such as an assistant pastor, deacon, or elder for men, or an older woman for a female) who can disciple and help you work through the concepts in this workbook. Ideally, now you have at least 3 persons from your church committed to helping you: a prayer partner, a TCF, and a church leader. You **cannot** walk through this alone. You need people to help you.

Write down the name of your pastor in the space provided: _____
_____

It is recommended that you commit to pray for your pastor at least once each week.

12. You are highly encouraged to begin a personal journal in a separate notebook. Get a separate notebook to utilize as a journal.

Yes, even men are encouraged to journal. Unfortunately, some people now view journaling as a strictly feminine activity; but in the past, men wrote in journals regularly. They wrote their thoughts to God, and chronicled their daily struggles and successes. Space will be provided in this workbook but you are strongly urged to have a personal journal as well to document your daily thoughts, ideas, attitudes, emotions, prayers, successes, failures, and desires.

It does not have to be a fancy, expensive, or large notebook. I recommend you designate a separate journal and pen to this study. This will help you and your trusted Christian friend (TCF) look at the matters of your heart in light of your current particular struggles. This is exciting because by journaling, you are creating a heritage that you might be able to share with your children and grandchildren or someone else in years to come. Write a prayer to God, some goals for the week, or thoughts from your daily Bible reading.

13. When you begin to meet with someone who is a leader in your church, ask that person how you can serve your local church.

One of the purposes of establishing this relationship is for your spiritual growth and discipleship. One way you will grow is by serving in your local church. Too many people come to church with a "serve me" attitude rather than a "how can I serve you?" attitude. Find appropriate opportunities to serve God in your local church. Write about these experiences in your journal.

14. Write down at least one or two goals that you want to accomplish from your study. What do you want to learn?

_____
_____
_____

Summary of Key Concepts from this chapter:
- *Turn to Christ for answers to your substance abuse problem (and any problem).*
- *Build a support system of Christians to help you face this difficult struggle in your life.*
- *Read and study God's Word to develop a biblical mindset for overcoming "addiction."*
- *Understand that real hope to overcome the problem is available and possible through Christ (Philippians 4:13).*

Section One: Teaching
Chapter 1: A Spiritual Problem

A wise man once told me: "You are not a body with a soul but you are a soul with a body." You are a spiritual creature with a soul that will live forever. Your physical body will deteriorate and die, but your soul will live eternally in one of two destinations: heaven or hell. This is according to the Bible in Matthew 25:46: **"And these will go away into eternal punishment, but the righteous into eternal life."**

Your soul is who you really are. I Samuel 16:7 tells us that man may look on the outward appearance but God looks at the heart: **"But the Lord said to Samuel, "Do not look on his appearance or on the height of his stature, because I have rejected him. For the Lord sees not as man sees: man looks on the outward appearance, but the Lord looks on the heart."** Since God looks at your heart, He knows your spiritual condition. Have you surrendered your life to His lordship today? _____

Does your heart want to control your life and control others or is your heart willing to surrender to Christ as your Head as you become part of His body? _____

Spiritual problems affecting the soul demand spiritual answers. In secular programs devoid of Christ, worldly wisdom is offered to the "addict" in the form of the idea of "addiction" as a "disease" with "no cure." It is not so with Christ and in the Bible. God offers our souls real hope in that "addiction" is called a sin of "idolatry" and "drunkenness" which requires confession, repentance, and faith in Christ to overcome. While there may be temptations to sin again, God has provided both the willingness and the power in Christ to say "no" to idolatry and to say "yes" to Christ. Philippians 2:13 states: **"for it is God who works in you, both to will and to work for his good pleasure."**

God provides the solution to our spiritual problem(s). The world offers helpful insights from time to time, but God provides answers in His Word and by the Holy Spirit.

1. Read the following Scriptures in your Bible aloud (alone and/or with your TCF). In your journal, summarize what the Scripture means. (Check off each as you read them and answer the questions that follow)

☐ Read and summarize **I Corinthians 1:18** in your journal.

Do you understand why the principles in this workbook will not make sense apart from a personal relationship with Jesus Christ? _____

The Heart of Addiction Workbook

Read Appendix B in The Heart of Addiction book, "The Gospel is 'Good News'" now whether you are a Christian or not. The Gospel is refreshing for Christians to read, too.

Unless you are born again, the Bible will seem like foolishness to you.

☐ Read and summarize **II Timothy 3:16-17** and **Matthew 22:29** in your journal.

Does God's Word equip you for "every good work," including overcoming substance abuse and addictions even though the words "substance abuse," "addiction," and "dependency" do not appear in the Bible? _____

Discuss with your TCF how the Bible equips you.

Does God understand your problem and has He spoken to you in an authoritative infallible way? _____ Is God silent on addiction? _____ Explain. _____
_____
_____
_____

☐ Read and summarize **Philippians 2:12-13**.

What does the partnership of the Holy Spirit in sanctification mean in relationship to how effective you will be in overcoming your struggle to sin?
_____
_____

Are you a Christian who has allowed your passion for God to diminish? _____
_____

If so, turn to Him now and ask for forgiveness. Repent by serving in your church or in some other organization as a volunteer. Taste and see that God and His Word and His promises of forgiveness in Christ Jesus are good. Psalm 34:8-10 says: **"Oh, taste and see that the Lord is good! Blessed is the man who takes refuge in him! Oh, fear the Lord, you his saints, for those who fear him have no lack! The young lions suffer want and hunger; but those who seek the Lord lack no good thing."**

What good things do you expect to experience and receive as a result of growing in Christ through obedience to God's commands? Discuss these with your TCF.

☐ Check when you have completed this.

> **I John 1:5-10** says:
>
> "This is the message we have heard from him and proclaim to you, that God is light, and in him is no darkness at all. If we say we have fellowship with him while we walk in darkness, we lie and do not practice the truth. But if we walk in the light, as he is in the light, we have fellowship with one another, and the blood of Jesus his Son cleanses us from all sin. If we say we have no sin, we deceive ourselves, and the truth is not in us. If we confess our sins, he is faithful and just to forgive us our sins and to cleanse us from all unrighteousness. If we say we have not sinned, we make him a liar, and his word is not in us."

What behaviors are typical for someone who is "walking in the darkness" of an "addiction"?

_____
_____
_____

What behaviors are typical for someone who is "walking in the light" (think of someone you know who is a truly committed Christian)?

_____
_____
_____

Are you beginning to walk in the light rather than in the darkness? _____

What principles from the Bible have you already learned?

_____
_____
_____

2. Complete the following ("fill in the blank").

These statements are found in *Chapter 1* of the <u>The Heart of Addiction</u>.

A. As a Christian who possesses a new heart and new identity in Christ, understand that "addiction" is a physical symptom of a deeper, spiritual problem of the attitudes of the heart generally called _____ in the Bible.

B. Specific to substance abuse, the Bible labels the effects of "addiction" as _____.

3. All persons have a worship disorder. In Chapter 1, "worship" is defined as "reverence offered a divine being." Worship is something you do. Worship is an action, thought, or word devoted to the "object" that is loved. The Lord Jesus Christ alone is to be the "object" of our affection.

Read **I Corinthians 10:31**. Write this verse in the space provided.

_____
_____

Idolatry is defined as "the worship of a physical object as a god." Idolatry is "immoderate" meaning there is no moderation in the devotion to the object. The object has been thought about, pursued, desired, and talked about excessively. The object has become the center of the universe in the idolater's eyes. The object has replaced Christ.

Christians, if we are not careful, are capable of falling into idolatry. We can avoid it by keeping our eyes upon Jesus. Read **I Corinthians 10:6-14** about the idolatry of God's children. Write down 3 key principles you observed in this passage of Scripture in the space provided:

_____
_____
_____

Be honest: what have you been thinking about, pursuing, and desiring more than God? List below:

_____
_____
_____
_____

Read **II Timothy 3:4** now.
Have you been a "lover of pleasure rather than a lover of God"?

_____

☐ Read **Romans 2:4** and **I John 1:9**.

Pray now and confess these idolatrous desires to God. Ask Him to forgive you through Christ Jesus who gave His life upon the cross. Ask God to grant you repentance (**Romans 2:4**) so that you can begin to worship Him alone.

4. What is a "heart" in the Bible? In the Bible, a "heart" is the spiritual, innermost part of a human being.

Fill in the blank: "Figuratively defined as the _____ or mind, as it is the fountain and seat of the thoughts, passions, desires, appetites, affections, purposes, endeavors."[3]

Write **Psalm 119:36** in the space provided:

_____
_____
_____

You are a wonderful mixture of a physical body and a spiritual body. When caught in "addiction," it is easy to focus primarily upon the physical elements of the problem. I urge you to submit yourself to the care of a primary physician to address your physical body and its concerns. I also urge you to submit yourself to the care of a trusted Christian friend (TCF) to address your spiritual soul and its concerns. In general, people are quick to go to the doctor for physical ailments but slow to go to a pastor for spiritual "ailments."

Call your TCF to ask for biblical counsel on how you can serve and worship God better.

5. Which path do you now choose to travel for the remainder of your life: God's or yours? _____

For Christians, life is challenging because there is an internal war waging between the "flesh" and the Holy Spirit.

☐ Read **Romans 7:21-25**.

For Christians, the challenge of living according to the Holy Spirit's leading may be exacerbated by the "fleshly" desires to seek pleasure and avoid pain. Your physical body is NOT to dictate to your spiritual body. Instead, your spiritual body is to dictate to your physical body. In other words, you are to live according to your new, spiritual person which is the indwelling of the Holy Spirit. Those persons that you know who are caught in the trap of active "addiction" and "idolatry" are living according to their physical desires called the "flesh." They are not under the power and authority of the Holy Spirit.

---

[3] Strong, J. 1996. The exhaustive concordance of the Bible: showing every word of the text of the common English version of the canonical books, and every occurrence of each word in regular order (electronic ed.). Woodside Bible Fellowship: Ontario.

The Heart of Addiction Workbook

Read and write **Ephesians 5:18** in the space provided: _____
_____

Read **Matthew 26:41** and **Mark 14:38**.
What do these parallel verses in the Gospels reveal about your physical body called the "flesh"?_____

Read **2 Corinthians 5:17: "Therefore, if anyone is in Christ, he is a new creation. The old has passed away; behold, the new has come."**

☐ Read **Ephesians 4:17-24**.
In this passage, God tells us that new believers in Christ are given a new nature and are to learn to live according to the "new man" rather than the "old man." As you read further, you will learn more about this biblical principle and how it applies to "addiction" and "idolatry."

Read **Colossians 3:1-10**.
"Setting your mind on things above" takes energy and effort from you. You have to "set your mind" on eternal things that feed your soul - not your flesh.

Read **Ephesians 5:18** again (you should have it written above).

Your challenge now is to feed your new, "spirit man" by reading, studying, memorizing, and meditating upon God's Word. The Holy Spirit works in partnership with the Word of God so the more you "feast upon the Word," the more you will grow spiritually by the power of Christ.

☐ Read these passages of Scripture about the Word of God:
John 1:1-14
Isaiah 55:10-11
Hebrews 4:12
James 1:21-23

> Walking down the path provided by the Lord God is difficult because you are to be a "doer" of His Word. Being a "doer" requires you to put the commands of His Word into action. You are to walk by faith and not by sight meaning you must trust in Christ to produce fruit in your spiritual person. Temptations and trials will come as you battle a

physical "addiction," but the battle is spiritual. Say "no" to the desires of your "flesh" which seek to please the body and begin saying "yes" to the desires of God. The road to self leads to destruction (**Ephesians 5:18 & Proverbs 13:15**).

The road to Jesus Christ leads to eternal prosperity and some blessings in this life. The blessings are spiritual fruit of the Spirit (**Galatians 5:22-23**). This "fruit" has temporal and eternal blessing.

☐ Read the following passages of Scripture about your eternal, spiritual soul and its destination:
I Peter 1:9
John 6:58
John 10:28
Titus 1:2
Titus 3:7.

Develop a heavenly mindset today! Begin practicing your worship of God today since as a Christian, you will worship Him in eternity forever.

Summary of Key Concepts from this chapter:
- ❖ *"Addiction" is a physical manifestation of a spiritual problem rooted in one's sinful nature.*
- ❖ *"Addiction" is better termed "idolatry" in the Bible.*
- ❖ *God's Word has answers for "addiction" though one must begin to understand biblical terms and concepts which provide real hope.*

The Heart of Addiction Workbook

Chapter 2: Man's Theories and God's Truth

1. What are the 6 resources discussed in the book that God has provided for the Christian?

- ❖ _____
- ❖ _____
- ❖ _____
- ❖ _____
- ❖ _____
- ❖ _____

2. Your Creator, God the Father, knows you quite well. Nothing is hidden from Him. Read Psalm 139.

Write verse 13 of Psalm 139 in the space provided: _____
_____
_____

3. You are dependent upon God for your every breath, for your being; but at the same time you can call on Him at all times, any time day or night. You can know Your Creator, God – the One Who made you – from what has been revealed about Him in the Bible.

Write a prayer to God asking Him to reveal Himself through the Holy Scriptures in a deeper and more meaningful way:
_____
_____
_____
_____

4. Apart from Christ, can you overcome your addiction by yourself?
_____

5. List the three unique characteristics [answers found in Chapter 2] that make the Bible matchless when compared to other books.
_____
_____
_____

6. Read the following Scriptures: *(Check off each as you read them and answer the questions that follow).*

☐ Read **2 Timothy 3:16-17**

What does "inspired" mean? _____

_____

These verses convey to us that God is the author of the Bible. Knowing that God is perfect and can be perfectly trusted, can you trust His Word? _____

☐ Read **2 Peter 1:3**

Can you trust His Word on the subject of addiction because addiction is included in "all things that pertain to life and godliness"? _____

Can you trust God? _____

☐ Read **John 3:16** and **I John 4:9-10**

Write down why God can be trusted based on these verses:

_____
_____
_____
_____

7. Have you ever wondered why Christian preachers sometimes disagree about important concepts in the Bible?

If so, here is the answer: Mankind has a sinful nature and often interprets Scriptures incorrectly. Every person has spiritual "blind spots" no matter how much he or she studies the Bible. There is nothing wrong with God. He, alone, is perfect. Mankind is not perfect and may wrongly interpret the meaning of God's Word at times. Unfortunately, no person is immune from error. Therefore, you have to be like a "Berean" in **Acts 17:10-11**.

☐ Read **Acts 17:10-11**.

They studied the Scriptures eagerly to make sure their leaders taught them correctly. You must do the same. It is your responsibility to grow in Christ. No one else can grow for you!

8. Write out how your sin nature has affected your own:

• Physical body

_____

_____

- Mental state (or thinking)
  _____
  _____

- Emotions
  _____
  _____

- Spiritual state
  _____
  _____

- Belief in who you are (in other words, what lies of your past are you believing about yourself?)
  _____
  _____

Being a Christian does not mean that you are perfect or "fixed." You will struggle. Even though you are a Christian, you will wrestle with your flesh, including the physical, mental, emotional, and spiritual things like those in your list above. But by the power of the Holy Spirit working in conjunction with your study of the Bible, you will be transformed physically, mentally, emotionally, and spiritually.

☐ Read **Romans 12:1-2**.

☐ What should you believe about who you are in Christ according to the Bible? (hint: read **2 Corinthians 5:17**)
_____
_____

☐ **9. Read Ezekiel 36:26-27** God gives you a new heart and places the Holy Spirit inside of you to empower you to comprehend His Word. God wants to "transform" you from a self-centered, or self-consumed, person with a sin nature that dominates you into a person who is led by the Holy Spirit; one who says what Jesus says at the end of **Luke 22:42**.

Read and write **Luke 22:42** out in the space provided. _____
_____
_____

10. List 3 to 5 practical ways that you can say "not my will, but Your will be done, Father, in my life."

_____
_____
_____
_____

11. Are you willing to do everything God requires to battle your addiction?

☐ Read **Proverbs 3:5-8**.

Are you committed to approaching addiction God's Way rather than in your own way? _____

Discuss these answers with your TCF.

12. Are you teachable when you read the Bible, when you hear preaching, and when you talk to your TCF? _____ Discuss this answer with your TCF.

13. Write out a brief prayer from your own heart asking God to help you to be open to His Word, the Holy Spirit's teaching, and to the feedback you receive from your TCF while you read <u>The Heart of Addiction</u>.

_____
_____
_____
_____

14. Complete Appendix E "The Extent of My Problem" found in <u>The Heart of Addiction</u> if you have not already done so.

15. With what idol have you been filling your God-given desire to worship God?

List the specific drugs, substances, people, pleasurable activities, or other idols in your heart that you have been addicted to:

_____
_____
_____
_____

16. What God-given responsibilities have you been willingly neglecting while pursuing fulfillment of the idolatrous desires for your idol? (i.e. failed to pay bills: list the specific bills, being specific about the lies you told, failed to love spouse, failed to love children, list other failures as well.)

_____
_____
_____
_____
_____

17. What immoral acts have you been (or are now) doing in order to fulfill your desire for your idol? (i.e. lying, failing to tell the truth, stealing, cheating, manipulating, blame-shifting, sexually immoral acts, list others) It is not fun to list these types of behaviors on paper but it is necessary at this time. **You do not have to be specific and do not list other person's names!** If you are uncomfortable about writing them out, then write them on a separate sheet of paper and then totally destroy it after you've prayed and asked the Lord to forgive you. The great news is that you can be forgiven of these sins by the Lord if you are a Christian! Write these sins in a general way:

_____
_____
_____
_____

Sadly, many persons caught in the trap of "active addiction," meaning they are continuing to use mind-altering substances excessively, view other people merely as *objects*. In other words, when one is abusing drugs and alcohol, people are viewed as one of two types of "objects." People who give the "active addict" what he/she wants are objects called "enablers." On the opposite end of the spectrum, people who deny the "active addict" what he/she wants are objects called "obstacles."[4]

---

[4] For more on the topic of viewing people as "objects," refer to chapter 1 of my book, <u>Divine Intervention: Hope and Help for Families of Addicts</u> published by Focus Publishing in Bemidji, MN, (1-800-91-FOCUS).

When you were involved in "active addiction," what people were "enablers" to you and what people were "obstacles" to you?

ENABLERS	OBSTACLES
_____	_____
_____	_____
_____	_____
_____	_____

You are beginning a transformation process according to **Romans 12:2** and **Ephesians 4:22-24**. It is not "recovery" but TRANSFORMATION.

Write down 3 ways that you want the Lord to transform you:

_____
_____
_____

18. *Choose today whether you will serve sin and the desires of your flesh OR whether you will serve the Lord by doing what is right. Write your answer in the space provided:* _____

The Bible tells us that a person will either present him/herself as a slave to righteousness or a slave to sin according to the biblical definition of "idolatry" and "addiction" in Romans 6:16-18: **"Do you not know that if you present yourselves to anyone as obedient slaves, you are slaves of the one whom you obey, either of sin, which leads to death, or of obedience, which leads to righteousness? But thanks be to God, that you who were once slaves of sin have become obedient from the heart to the standard of teaching to which you were committed, and, having been set free from sin, have become slaves of righteousness."** You are encouraged to embrace your slavery to righteousness by living an abundant and obedient life unto God your wise Creator and loving Father.

19. *Read Appendix A in The Heart of Addiction book now.*

Compare your experiences with secular self-help groups to your experiences with the church. Admittedly, some churches do a poor job of helping those who struggle with substance abuse; however, that sad assessment seems to be changing. Maybe the Lord is calling you to start a small Bible study at your church focused upon "addiction." Ask a trustworthy, willing leader of your church to teach a small, support group for "addiction" using these materials. You can be a co-leader or helper and watch the Lord use you to transform others in Christ.

Summary of Key Concepts from this chapter:

- *While mankind offers limited insights for "addiction," when rightly interpreted, God's Word offers the best insights and real answers because He is the Creator of the "addict."*
- *The biblical approach to "addiction" is NOT a "disease concept" but addresses the "sinful nature" of mankind. Jesus Christ died for our sins and we can become new creations in Christ (2 Corinthians 5:17).*
- *God's Word says that we are to be "transformed", which is not a "recovery process" but a total restructuring of our lives. We become new in Christ and have a new identity in Christ.*

Chapter 3: Redefining the World's Terminology

Let us be clear about our terminology. Substance abuse and addiction manifest as a physical problem but the root issues are in the spiritual realm of one's own heart. This deep spiritual problem of the heart is called "idolatry" in the Bible. In this workbook, the terms "substance abuse" and "substance abuser" are utilized at times. Also, the words "addict" and "addiction" are utilized because this is the terminology that most people in the world understand. In this chapter, those secular terms are re-defined to embrace biblical thinking on this topic. As a Christian who possesses a new heart and new identity in Christ, you must understand that "addiction" is a physical symptom of a deeper, spiritual problem of the heart called "idolatry" in the Bible.

In fact, the word "idolatry" can be extended to include various "pleasures" like drugs, alcohol, sex, food, gambling, sleep, television, internet, exercise, sports, and video games, just to name a few! II Timothy 3:4 identifies persons who desire an idolatrous pleasure more than they desire to honor God as **"lovers of pleasure rather than lovers of God."** These people are pleasure-centered rather than Christ-centered. The idolatry of substance abuse, addiction, and drunkenness is not a new problem to the Lord. Specifically, this book addresses the sins related to substance abuse and a physical "addiction" to drugs and alcohol. However, the biblical principles for overcoming a substance abuse problem also apply to the various idolatrous pleasures listed above since those pleasures can be experienced excessively, can cause one to neglect his or her responsibilities, and can lead to devastating consequences.

1. Would you say that your problems with the sin of drunkenness were a result of a compulsive urge (an uncontrollable desire)? (Yes or No)

Do you now see that you are responsible for developing your habits? _____

2. The use of the word "compulsive" allows you to do at least 5 negative things. Name them here:

_____
_____
_____
_____

3. Define the following terms with the information that you have learned from the text.

- Irrational:

- Irresistible:

- Compulsive:

- Habits:

4. Habits are not broken, they are replaced.
Write one "bad habit" that you have and write a "good habit" with which you could replace it.

BAD HABIT _____

_____

GOOD HABIT (replacement) _____

_____

5. What kind of habits are you currently practicing: godly ones to serve Christ or ungodly ones to serve yourself? _____

Read **1 Timothy 4:7b-8** and write it out in the space provided: _____

_____

Read **Romans 6:16-19**.

Are you "presenting your body" to drugs and alcohol which will enslave you? _____

List 3 ways you plan to "present your body" to righteousness.

_____
_____
_____

6. Write out the new definition of addiction as redefined by the author at the end of chapter 3.

_____
_____

7. God is not as interested in your happiness as He is in your holiness. By being holy, you will likely become happier though not always. What do these statements prioritize: holiness (obedience to Christ) OR happiness (obedience to pleasing oneself temporarily)?

8. Write down an encouraging verse(s) to begin memorizing.
_____
_____
_____

Summary of Key Concepts from this chapter:
- ❖ *"Addiction" is not compulsive, though it looks that way. Rather, it is "habitual" and the Bible practically speaks to replacing habits.*
- ❖ *"Addiction" redefined with biblical constructs is the "persistent, habitual use of a substance known by the user to be harmful."*
- ❖ *Bad habits can be replaced with godly habits with the help of the Holy Spirit and the practical wisdom of God's Word.*

Chapter 4: Who Are You?

1. Read Hebrews 4:12-13.

Think about this analogy. Who knows more about your automobile: the manufacturer who created and built it OR a mechanic who works on it? While the mechanic knows some of the facts about your car, the manufacturer who created it knows all the finer details of it. Further, the best mechanics study the manufacturer's descriptions of the car's design. God is your Creator and He really does know every detail about you and your life. Therefore, God knows what you need and His Word speaks to your real needs.

2. If you have not done so already, use Appendix E in *The Heart of Addiction* book to help determine the extent of your problem.

3. Ask yourself: Am I enslaved in my addiction within every area of my life (marital, economic, social, physical, emotional, familial, occupational, and spiritual areas)? _____ Or am I an occasional abuser who excessively consumes a mood-altering substance? _____

4. Ask yourself: what areas of my life have been affected by my substance abuse?
_____
_____
_____

5. Categorize yourself in the following manner: (circle one)
(a) I am a believer, trusting in the Lord Jesus Christ alone for salvation.
(b) I am an unbeliever, doubting that my sins have been forgiven.

6. Now, categorize your problem in the following manner: (circle one)
(a) I am an occasional abuser of a substance to excess.
(b) I am a life-dominated (or frequent) abuser of a substance to excess.

Note: The life-dominated abuser is often called physically "dependent upon the substance" because when the substance is not used, this person experiences physical withdrawal symptoms.

7. Regardless of the category in which you find yourself in #6 above, the problem of excessive substance abuse is a sin issue of the heart that must be radically changed.

Changing from pleasing self to pleasing and serving God is a focus upon proper worship. Ask the Lord to give you strength because you cannot have lasting victory by relying only on your own strength - regardless of whether you are a drunkard or an occasional abuser. Ask your TCF to help you in your transformation process today.

8. What are three of the biblical terms for addiction, occasional substance abuse, or chemical dependency? (Hint: Read on!)

_____
_____
_____

9. God labels this behavior as idolatry, drunkenness, and sin. Sin is the bad news, but the good news is that the Lord Jesus Christ died for sinners who repent and put their trust in Christ alone for eternal life.

If you are not a Christian and you want to be a Christian, you can become a child of the kingdom of God here on earth and begin to experience the transforming power of God during this present lifetime. You must be "born again". This term is referring to the regenerating power of the Holy Spirit. Read Appendix B now.

10. Read I Corinthians 4:20 regarding God's kingdom: "For the kingdom of God does not consist in talk but in power."

It is time to quit talking about the sin problem. It is time to repent and to begin to deal with the sin of drunkenness in practical ways as someone who is walking in the kingdom of God. Write down one thing that you can DO today to demonstrate true repentance and faith in God to overcome your addiction.

_____

11. Your Creator wants you to have a meaningful, radical relationship with Him. You can pray and talk to Him anytime. Also, you can listen to Him anytime when you read the Bible. Spend at least 15 minutes each day in Bible reading and prayer. Develop this "quiet time" habit to get your mind centered upon Christ.

Ask your TCF, church leader, and/or prayer partner to begin a study of the Bible with you through a particular book of the Bible. The gospel of John is recommended but Genesis, Ephesians, Philippians, Colossians, and Proverbs are fine, too. You really cannot go wrong with studying God's Word with a loved one!

12. List 10 people to contact and ask the following question: "Would you say that I have been a godly, Christian person or a selfish person?" Contact each one and ask them to be honest with their assessment. Be prepared to hear bad news if you have been mired in an addiction. Use the lines below to list each name and the response.

_____   _____
_____   _____
_____   _____
_____   _____
_____   _____

13. If you have not already, ask your TCF if he/she thinks that you have been "sincerely deceived" or have been a case of "mistaken identity." Though your TCF does not know your heart, he or she can assess the fruit you have been producing. "Am I a Christian?" is the most important question you will ever ask yourself. "God, will you save me from my sins based upon the sacrifice of Jesus Christ?" is the most important question you will ever ask God.

Note: Even if people cannot see the fruit in your new life, your goal cannot be to please people. You must seek to please the Lord first. The above questions are designed to open your eyes to how you have been acting and how others have perceived you. If you have recently surrendered to Christ, then tell each person your good news and ask them to forgive you for any sins you may have committed against them. This is an excellent opportunity to grow in Christ though it will be difficult.

Summary of Key Concepts from this chapter:

- *Your identity is no longer in your "sin" but in Christ if you have asked the Lord Jesus Christ to be your Lord and Savior.*
- *For this reason, you do not have to daily confess being an "addict" or "alcoholic" because you are not identified by your sin but by the righteousness of Christ.*
- *The Lord desires for you to know Him intimately.*

Chapter 5: Frequently Asked Questions

1. The following are some thoughts that you may have had at times in the past or are currently having. Using this list, put a check mark next to the thoughts that you have experienced:

"I want to feel good right now."

"I am living for the moment and will worry about the consequences of my choices later."

"I want to feel good temporarily so I am going to use this drug or alcohol."

"It's got to be better than what I feel right now."

"It will be a nice escape."

"I cannot stop thinking about it."

"I close my eyes and I can still see it."

"I go to a quiet place and it calls my name. I can smell and taste it."

"I know it's wrong, but I want to do it anyway."

"I feel so out of control."

"I pray but it doesn't go away. I pray and nothing changes."

"I've done everything that I know to do. Oh, God, where are You when I need You?"

"There's no way out of the slavery of addiction."

Write down any other thoughts that you have had that were not listed above.

_____
_____
_____

2. Write down any questions about yourself or your addiction that you would like to ask God to answer.

_____
_____
_____

3. Do any of the questions you have written down on your list above match the questions that the author listed in this chapter? List them:

_____
_____
_____

4. Read 2 Timothy 3:16-17 again. Would you say that God has the answers you need for your life and wants you to better know His character, power, and wisdom?

_____

5. Does God's Word still seem foreign and far off to you? _____

If you answered 'yes', seek the prayerful help of your TCF to discuss your answer to this question.

☑ Read **Psalm 119:18**.

☐ If you have not done so already, read Appendix B.

Pray right now that God will open your eyes to see His Wonderful glory and His ways and His truth applied to your life.

If you answered 'no', then pray right now and pour out your heart of thanksgiving for the wonderful things you are seeing in His law. Pray that your hunger for His Word will continue to grow. Pray that you will be sanctified by the truth. His Word is truth (**John 17:17**). That is my prayer for you. Your Savior prayed for *you* in **John 17:20-21** and continues to pray and make intercession for you before God. Read **John 17:20-21** now.

6. In what specific ways are you currently hindering (or have you in the past hindered) the Holy Spirit's power to change you?

_____
_____
_____
_____

7. What can you do differently (from #6 above) now?

_____
_____
_____
_____

8. Do you understand the light switch analogy near the end of this chapter?

_____

If you enjoy visual things, in the space provided, try sketching a depiction of this metaphor so that you will have a mental picture of how much you can help or hinder God's work in your life.

The Heart of Addiction Workbook

9. Do you relate to the downward spiral staircase analogy? _____

Isn't it good news that the staircase goes back up for the believer with every step of obedience? Try sketching a visual representation (it does not have to be an artistic masterpiece) of this concept as you relate to it and apply it to your life:

It will be beneficial to look back at these notes and illustrations later down the path of your transformation with the Lord. Just think, God will give you the opportunity to help others in their struggle with addiction one day and your notes may be a great encouragement to them as well as to you.

10. Read Romans 12:2. Rather than "conform" to the world's approach to addiction, the Holy Spirit promises to "transform" you like a caterpillar into a butterfly when you read, study, memorize, apply, and meditate upon the Scriptures. In your journal, write about what that means to you now and will mean to your future.

Summary of Key Concepts from this chapter:
- ❖ *The Lord knows your questions even before you ask and has provided many answers for "addiction" and "idolatry" in His Word.*
- ❖ *You need His help to see clearly. Christ provides the power to overcome any "addiction."*
- ❖ *You do not need "will power" but the "will of God power" provided to you in Christ.*

Chapter 6: The Good Purpose of Drugs and Alcohol

1. What is the biblical purpose of alcohol and drugs according to Proverbs 31:6-7 and I Timothy 5:23? _____
_____
_____
_____

2. Have you ever longed to "be able to drink just a little" and "enjoy alcohol like 'normal' people do"? Read Matthew 5:29-30.

Jesus is teaching us to be radical about our Christian walk. Jesus is not teaching us to literally pluck our eye out or to amputate our arm. Jesus is shockingly instructing us to remove anything in our lives that would cause us to sin. Examine your life honestly and ask yourself: Would the moderate use of alcohol and/or drugs cause me to sin by excessively using these substances to the point of being out of control? If so, then do you now realize that once you overcome your sin of drunkenness, you may never be able to go back to the days of "social drinking" and moderate drinking? _____

Does that make you sad? _____ Discuss your answer honestly with your TCF.

3. Make a list of the pros and cons of the "radical amputation" of alcohol and drugs from your life.

PROS	CONS

4. How are you preparing your heart and life for this radical obedience? On the next page, list the thoughts you are having when you think about living this radical lifestyle and the sacrifices you are called by God to make. Be honest and discuss with your TCF.

The Heart of Addiction Workbook

_____
_____
_____
_____

5. If you have not done so already, complete Appendix C: Sample Put Off and Put On Lists in <u>The Heart of Addiction</u> book.

6. Based upon your answers from Appendix C, make a specific plan today about how you will remove yourself from the people, places, and things that might tempt you to use drugs and alcohol again.

List the pros and cons of these decisions. Discuss this with your TCF.

PROS   CONS

_____   _____
_____   _____
_____   _____
_____   _____
_____   _____
_____   _____

Consider sharing your lists and plan with your prayer partner, too, so that you may go before Our Lord in prayer for His strength to execute your plan.

Summary of Key Concepts from this chapter:
- ❖ *Alcohol is a drug in liquid form. Alcohol and drugs were created for a good purpose of relieving physical suffering, but have been misused for the purpose of relieving spiritual suffering.*
- ❖ *Spiritual suffering is designed to lead us back to Christ in humble brokenness, repentance, and submission.*
- ❖ *God may be calling you to "radically obey" Him by "amputating" chemicals and drugs from your life.*

Chapter 7: Drunkenness

1. Who was the first person recorded in the Bible (Genesis 9) to become drunk with wine? _____ *What were the consequences of this drunken event?* _____

2. Who was the second person recorded in the Bible (Genesis 19) to become drunk with wine? _____ *What were the consequences of this drunken event?* _____
_____

3. Are you doubting your salvation and security in Christ Jesus?
Remember that substance abuse treatment centers cannot change your heart. Consequences like prison, near death car accidents, and divorce cannot change your heart. Family members cannot change your heart. I cannot change your heart. You cannot change my heart. Who can change a sinner's heart? Who can change a sinning Christian's heart? Obviously, you know the answer has to be God alone.

Some addicts want God to fix their old, sinful heart, but that is a wrong idea. God has a better plan. He wants to give you a new heart, a new nature, and a new identity. Remember that **Ezekiel 36:26-27** says that God not only redeems His people, but God *empowers* His people by giving them a new nature and a new heart: **"And I will give you a new heart, and a new spirit I will put within you. And I will remove the heart of stone from your flesh and give you a heart of flesh. And I will put my Spirit within you, and cause you to walk in my statutes and be careful to obey my rules."**

The old heart is removed so Christians have one new heart and one new nature. Now, with a new nature, Christians have the power to *choose* to do either what is right or wrong. Persons who are *not* born again believers in Christ Jesus do not have the indwelling power of the Holy Spirit to enable them to make right choices that please God. Sinners make selfish choices even if a choice *appears* to be unselfish. God says sinners' hearts are "deceitfully wicked" (**Jeremiah 17:9**) meaning that while some actions of sinners appear to be "good," the intent of the sinner's heart was for selfish gain. This teaching is difficult for some to comprehend because we like to believe that some people are good and others are bad; however, everyone is born with a sinful nature that is "deceitful" in that it misleads and tricks us into thinking that we are good. God says that no one is righteous or good apart from Him.

The Heart of Addiction Workbook

There are two possibilities here: either you are a believer or you are an unbeliever. You must not attempt to go any further in this study if you are not resting in Christ alone for your eternal salvation. Are you doubting whether or not you have this new heart? Turn to Appendix B now if you have doubts.

4. Have you ever wondered: "If I have a new heart and nature, then why do I continue to struggle with sin?" _____

Christians must know their identity is in Christ even though they struggle with the temptation to sin everyday. Read **Romans 8:9**: **"You, however, are not in the flesh but in the Spirit, if in fact the Spirit of God dwells in you. Anyone who does not have the Spirit of Christ does not belong to him."** Christians have the Holy Spirit living inside of them. Christians are in the Spirit and not in the flesh; however, the problem is that Christians can still live "according to the flesh" instead of living "according to the Spirit." God wants you to yield to the Holy Spirit's leading rather than yielding to your own selfish desires. God wants you to say, "not *my* will but *Your* will be done, Father God." God loves you and wants to lead you down the path He has planned for you, rather than letting you take your own path that leads to destruction. Read **Proverbs 3:5-7** again. God gives you the indwelling power of the Holy Spirit along with a new heart.

Do you know that your identity is in Christ alone? _____

Do you recognize how knowing who you are in Christ can help you to overcome your "addiction"? _____

Christ is in you and you are in Christ. Discuss this concept and your above answers with your TCF.

5. Is it possible to have a new heart but still desire an "escape" using alcohol and drugs? Yes, even though a Christian possesses a new heart and new nature, the *majority* of Christians who struggle with excessive substance abuse still battle a desire for their drug of choice. It is a physical consequence. God does not automatically zap your body into right feeling and your mind into right thinking; it is a gradual transformation process.

The new heart's desire is to stay clean and sober to please God, but early in the process there is a difficult struggle due to past habit patterns and real, physiological cravings. Don't let these struggles cause you to become discouraged because this process of fighting your addictive habits and cravings is very difficult at first. It is an opportunity to depend upon God and to trust Him. Write out a brief prayer asking

God to help you replace your addictive habits with godly habits that please Him and transform you into the likeness of Christ.

___
___
___
___

6. The new heart God gives you is alive but it needs your attention. You must continually fill it up with God's Word and the Holy Spirit.

To illustrate: think of the continual filling up of your new heart just as you would think of filling a pitcher of iced tea. You fill up the pitcher with tea. After the tea is poured out and the pitcher is empty, you must fill up the pitcher again. The process is repeated over and over. Filling yourself up with the Word of God is a continual process rather than a one-time event. When you fill up your heart with the Word of God, you give the Holy Spirit more resources to increase the amount of His power working in your heart and life. God did not just give you a container, like the tea pitcher, to fill up: you *are* the container referred to as "earthen vessel" in the Scriptures. Sketch a drawing to illustrate this pitcher analogy in the space provided:

7. Develop a plan to make time each day to read and study God's Word. Use Appendix F in <u>The Heart of Addiction</u> book to help you restructure your daily schedule.

8. Pick out at least one of these verses of Scripture to memorize: Colossians 3:16, Ephesians 5:18, or 2 Corinthians 4:7.

Write down the verse you selected on a 3" x 5" index card or small piece of paper. Put it in your pocket or purse so that you can retrieve it during the day. Throughout the day, pull out the card with your handwritten verse and read it over and over to memorize it. Do this for one full week. By the end of the week, begin to meditate on the verse in depth. Think about what that verse means and how you can apply it to your life in practical ways.

The Heart of Addiction Workbook

9. The new heart must be cultivated by you just as a gardener cultivates a garden.

A gardener works hard to pull weeds, fertilize the soil, water the plants, and protect the garden. In His sovereign grace, God gives you the new heart and provides the indwelling of the Holy Spirit; however, you are *responsible* for cultivating your new heart like a gardener tends his flowers, and a farmer cultivates his field for farming. The farmer prepares the field by breaking up and loosening the hard ground for the purpose of growing crops. Can the farmer make the crops grow? No. God makes the crops grow, but the farmer cultivates the field and provides the best opportunity for the crops to grow.[5]

Farming is difficult work. Like the farmer, you must put forth some very hard work to attack your addiction by "putting off" your "old self" and by "putting on" your "new self."[6] Read **Colossians 3:9-10: "Do not lie to one another, seeing that you have put off the old self with its practices and have put on the new self, which is being renewed in knowledge after the image of its creator."** Your new heart gives you the *will* that desires to please God and to "put off" your "old self with its practices," but it is not a magic pill or quick fix for the problem of what the Bible calls your "old self." You have a new desire, placed inside you by God, to deny the desires of the "old self" with its selfish, sinful, and familiar habit patterns of thinking, speaking, and acting.

As you read further in the book, more details will be given about how you are to "go to war" against the tendency to fall back into the sinful mode of thinking, speaking, and acting on a *daily* basis.

10. How can you begin to break up and loosen the hardened ground of your heart so that God's Word will be planted in you?

List 1 specific thing you will start doing today that will cultivate your heart for God.

_____

11. While it is easy and tempting to go back to what is familiar, God expects you, as one of His redeemed people, to:

- exercise faith in Him
- by doing the hard work of this new way of life
- in thanksgiving to Him
- for His redeeming of your soul and paying the penalty for your sins.

---

[5] Reeder, Harry, "Transformed by Truth. Cultivating a Heart for God: How to Cultivate a Heart for God," sermon series preached at Briarwood Presbyterian Church on October 30, 2005.

[6] Some translations call one's "old self" the "old man." Don't let these terms confuse you since they mean the same thing.

Drunkenness

The familiar patterns of the past are comfortable in the sense that the pain is known and expected. **Some Christians who struggle with drunkenness would prefer to stay in the prison of the pain of the known past, rather than to experience the freedom and liberty of living for Christ by faith.** This mentality is voluntary slavery when one lives according to his old nature. The prison cell's door is wide open, yet the addict chooses to remain in prison to his desires for the substance of choice.

As you repent and live for Jesus, what hard work can you expect to face as you begin to put-off and put-on? List 3 examples:

_____
_____
_____

Discuss these answers with your TCF in depth.

12. Living by faith and growing in grace is often referred to as "sanctification."

What is significant about growing in Christ by God's grace is that you are not expected to be perfect, but you *are* expected to be nauseated by your own failed attempts to overcome your sin. Do your failures and struggles with substance abuse and addiction make you sick? __Yes_____

Do you hate it? __Yes_____

The measure of a Christian is not by how much he sins, but by how much he repents!

13. Are you still in the prison of your selfish desires for your substance even though the prison door is wide open? __NO__

Explain specifically how this relates to your life. How did you choose (or how are you currently choosing) to stay in the situations that prevent your success at overcoming drunkenness? _____

How are you planning to choose to stay out of those situations that could tempt you to drunkenness?

_____
_____
_____

14. What are some of your earthly reminders and/or consequences of your sins?

_____
_____
_____

15. How can you see God's hand of grace and mercy in this earthly reminder or consequence of your sinful actions?

_____
_____
_____

If you are having trouble seeing God's grace in these consequences, ask your TCF to help you.

16. Are you still struggling with obeying God despite your new heart?
_____

What does this tell you about the battle with addiction? _____

17. When the Christian addict wants to change, he/she will do everything possible to try to change. Are you doing all you can to change? _____

It is effort that God desires from His people. Are you willing to change even if it hurts?
_____

Does your new heart hate your sin because it affects your relationship and your closeness to Christ? _____

Hating what God hates is evidence of being a true believer in Christ. You ought to feel guilty when you give in to your sin of addiction because the Holy Spirit is convicting you to bring about change in your life that is more pleasing to God. The Lord lovingly chastens His children, so you must receive the conviction of the Holy Spirit as loving discipline from your Heavenly Father who cares enough about you to be brutally honest with you.

☐ Read **Hebrews 12:5-7**.

18. Are you being more obedient to God and cultivating your new heart for Him? _____ Are you guarding your new heart and not allowing your "old self" with all of that terrible, negative thinking to influence your current behavior? _____

If so, how are you accomplishing this? _____
_____

19. Many defeated Christians fail to cultivate their new heart for Christ by neglecting Bible study, prayer, fellowship, serving others, corporate worship, and hearing the faithful preaching of the Word of God. Which of these vital activities is prominent in your life and which of these are you neglecting? _____
_____
_____

Whether you feel like doing these things or not is irrelevant at this point. You just need to do them. Live according to God's rules and not your own. Do the things mentioned above to cultivate your heart, even if you think they are not going to be fun and you dread doing them. For right now, just do them because it pleases God. Obedience to God is all that is required at this point. Willingness will come. Talk to your TCF honestly about your struggles with willingness and obedience.

20. Are you becoming more joyful even if your circumstances are not changing? _____

List 3 thoughts you can tell yourself to choose to be joyful in your state of mind leading to contentment and peace. Use the Bible to develop these thoughts. To get started, read **Philippians 4:8**.

_____
_____
_____

21. Are you getting "addicted" to learning about Jesus? _____

If not, then talk to your TCF and study the Gospels in your Bible some more. Give it time, but keep in mind, time without study will not profit you much.

22. Tell your TCF of your decision to become obedient to God even though you don't feel like it.

Ask your TCF and your prayer support persons to continue to pray with you that willingness and joy will come to your heart soon.

23. Using your own Bible, review all the Scriptures referenced in this section of the workbook and in the chapter you just read in the text.

24. In the space below, write a prayer to your Heavenly Father regarding these things you have just explored.

Pour out your heart in honest confession to your Creator who knows all things. **"Oh give thanks to the Lord, for he is good, for his steadfast love endures forever! Let the redeemed of the Lord say so, whom he has redeemed from trouble"** **(Psalm 107:1-2).**

_____
_____
_____
_____
_____
_____
_____
_____

Summary of Key Concepts from this chapter:
- ❖ *While "drunkenness" and "idolatry" might be new names and concepts to you, they are not new problems to God.*
- ❖ *"The heart of your problem is a problem with your heart."*
- ❖ *Do not compare yourself to others but compare yourself to Jesus Christ who is the standard. The law of God's Word shows us our need for a Savior.*

Chapter 8: The Depiction of Substance Abuse from Proverbs 23

1. If you are relating to the person described in Proverbs 23, thank God that He has chosen to reveal your sinful nature to you that you may turn and forsake your sin and be forgiven because of the work of Jesus Christ in His perfect obedience and death on the cross. Write out a thankfulness prayer to Him now:

_____
_____
_____

2. Read Proverbs 28:13. What thoughts and actions might you be covering up and need to confess to the Lord today? _____
_____
_____
_____

The Lord knows all of your thoughts! Confess them to Him now. Pray and ask the Lord to forgive you of those sins.

3. Develop a plan to begin "forsaking" those sins (not doing them anymore) according to Proverbs 28:13. Write out your practical plan now:

_____
_____
_____

Discuss your plan with your TCF.

4. Do you accept full responsibility for your sinful choices related to this problem? _____

5. Write out Proverbs 23:29-35. Summarize each verse in your own words.

_____
_____
_____
_____
_____
_____

Summary of Key Concepts from this chapter:
- *Drunkenness is a manifestation of a selfish heart and leads to destruction (Ephesians 5:18).*
- *Sin is deceptive because it looks like a minor problem though it takes us down a path of death and destruction.*
- *Confession and the forsaking (repenting) of sins are keys to unlocking God's blessing in our lives.*

Chapter 9: The Physical Components of Addiction

1. Define the following terms with the information you have now learned in this chapter:
- ❖ Appetite: _____
- ❖ Instinct: _____
- ❖ Cravings: _____
- ❖ Tolerance: _____

2. What are the 5 appetites mentioned by the author in this chapter?
_____
_____
_____
_____
_____

3. What is one more God-given appetite in every person? _____

4. If you have not done so already, list the name of a primary care physician to contact soon: _____

You should be under the care of a physician!

Summary of Key Concepts from this chapter:
- ❖ *Appetites are God-given and enable us to sustain our lives.*
- ❖ *Inordinate filling of physical appetites leads to idolatry.*
- ❖ *Worship is a spiritual appetite only satisfied in Christ.*

Chapter 10: Idolatry

1. Write the definition of "idolatry" given in this chapter: _____
_____

2. Can Christians allow themselves to become enslaved to idolatry? ___
_____
_____

Read I Corinthians 10:7.

3. Read Ephesians 2:10. According to this verse, why did God create you?
_____

4. Did you read the "stop button" and "go button" analogies? At times, did it seem to you that you have been or were pushing a "go button" for your drug of choice (alcohol is included as a drug)? _____

5. The "go button" analogy is a helpful way to remember that you are responsible for your choices. Are you doing everything you can to change your thoughts, motives, and actions? _____

Discuss this with your TCF soon and ask for honest feedback and suggestions.

6. Why were you enslaved to idolatry?
_____
_____
_____

7. Are you using your "go button" to worship the Lord now?

By worship, I do not just mean going to church on Sunday. By worship, I mean:
- Are you thinking about God throughout your day? _____
- Are striving to please God daily? _____
- Do you listen to godly music throughout your day? _____

- Are you meditating upon Scripture throughout your day? _____
- Do you pray at various times throughout your day? _____
- Do you read your Bible daily? _____

8. God knew that mankind, in his fallen state of sin, utilizes a variety of temporary pleasures to fulfill the desire to worship God. God calls it "idolatry." When you have your mind set upon experiencing a particular pleasure so much that you are:

- **willing to neglect** your God-given responsibilities and you are
- **willing to commit immoral acts (sins)** that you would not have normally done in order to obtain that temporary pleasure, then you are guilty of idolatry according to the Bible.

In what ways were you neglecting your God-given responsibilities?
_____
_____

In what ways are you now meeting those God-given responsibilities?
_____
_____

Discuss this with your TCF.

9. Physical addiction occurs when someone repeatedly satisfies a natural appetite and desire with a temporary pleasure containing addictive properties. In time, the person becomes a servant of the temporary object of pleasure rather than its master. Substance abuse and addiction are likened to slavery and idolatry in the Bible. You may have started using the substance of choice by having control over it, but it eventually overwhelmed you and you became a slave to the idol of pleasure. List some of the ways that your addictive behavior controlled your:

a) Thoughts _____
b) Emotions _____
c) Will and/or desires _____
d) Behaviors/actions (i.e. crimes committed, lies told) _____

10. Explain the "expediency principle" from I Corinthians 6:12 and I Corinthians 10:23 and how it applies to substance abuse.
_____
_____

11. Explain the idea of "radical amputation" of drugs and alcohol from Matthew 5:27-30 and how it applies to substance abuse:
_____
_____
_____

12. If you have been pushing your "go button," describe what God intends you to do instead: _____

13. What specific gifts has your Creator given you that will enable you to accomplish the purpose He has uniquely given to you?
_____
_____

14. What specific weaknesses of yours will He use in you to further glorify His name in all the earth?
_____
_____

Summary of Key Concepts from this chapter:
- ❖ *"Idolatry" is defined as "the worship of a physical object as a god" or "immoderate attachment or devotion to something."*
- ❖ *God holds every person accountable for their thoughts and actions.*
- ❖ *"Push your go button" for the Lord and not for your selfish pleasures.*

Chapter 11: The Perishing Mentality

1. What is a "perishing mentality"?
_____
_____

2. What does your "perishing mentality" consist of?
_____
_____

Ask your TCF for help or a loved one who knows you very well to give you insight.

3. How have you often tried to escape your life's problems?
_____
_____
_____

Was it discouraging when you failed to escape permanently? _____

Do you think you were trying to escape in your own strength and in your own way OR were you trying to escape God's way? _____

4. What were some of the small choices long ago that led you down the path of destruction?
_____
_____
_____

Do you see yourself today as completely responsible for the choices you made then?
_____

5. In your own words, ask God for forgiveness for those unwise choices you made which led you to a lifestyle of sin, drunkenness, and idolatry.

The Heart of Addiction Workbook

Write your confession and prayer here:
___
___
___

6. Explain how diagnostic terms like "disease" and even "addiction" can sometimes perpetuate the "victim mentality" and hinder your growth in Christ.
___
___

7. Summarize Psalm 55 in your own words without changing the meaning of the Scriptures.
___
___
___

8. Have you ever embraced a label or diagnosis of your sin condition that was unbiblical? ___

What was the term? ___

You must take responsibility for your sin. Confession of the sin of drunkenness is the direct opposite of the victim mentality that rules the world right now. Examples of this are verbalized in the following ways:

"It's not my fault; it's a **disease**."

"It's not my fault; it's Satan's/a **demon's attack** on me."

"It's not my fault; it's **my co-dependency**."

The embracing of these diagnostic labels result in one being angry at God because the line of thinking is: "God wired me this way. It is ultimately His fault that I am addicted and have this disease. I didn't ask for it."

Have you ever felt angry at God, thinking that He had "wired you" in this way?
___
___

The truth of the matter is that the sin of Adam resulted in your "fallen," sinful nature. Adam is not only to blame because you have made sinful choices leading to your destructive ways. The good news is that God is a Redeemer and He makes good out of our bad choices. How can you now seek to glorify God in this life by worshiping Him?

_____
_____
_____

9. The good news of the gospel is that Jesus Christ died for sin – for YOUR sin. You must ask for His forgiveness – then you can be forgiven.

In order to do that you must take full responsibility for your sin. You must not differentiate between your intentional and unintentional sin. You must take responsibility for **all** your actions. You cannot go any further until you do. Again, read **Proverbs 28:13**, which instructs you to confess AND forsake your sin. Putting off is only half the battle. The answer is not in just saying "No," but turning and running to the "Yes!" You have been living a selfish and isolated life. So now you must start talking to God – through prayer – and listening to God through the reading of his Word.

Write a prayer from your heart now asking God to help you see how it was your choice to push the "go button" for sin, and ask Him to cause you to replace your desires with the desire to worship Him.

_____
_____
_____

10. Do the following two things:

• Implement a journal if you have not already done so in which you talk to God. This is not just where you relate and list events that happened. Talk to God. Write down your prayers in that journal.

• Read the Bible multiple times throughout the day. Plan specific times to read the Bible for just a few minutes. Write those times down here. _____

The Heart of Addiction Workbook

Just as gasoline FUELS an automobile, the "Perishing Mentality" is FUELED by one's thinking as depicted in the diagram below. The prideful, self-focused messages that you tell yourself will drive you right off a cliff of destruction IF you do not put-off those thoughts and replace them with humble, biblical truths about who you are in Christ.

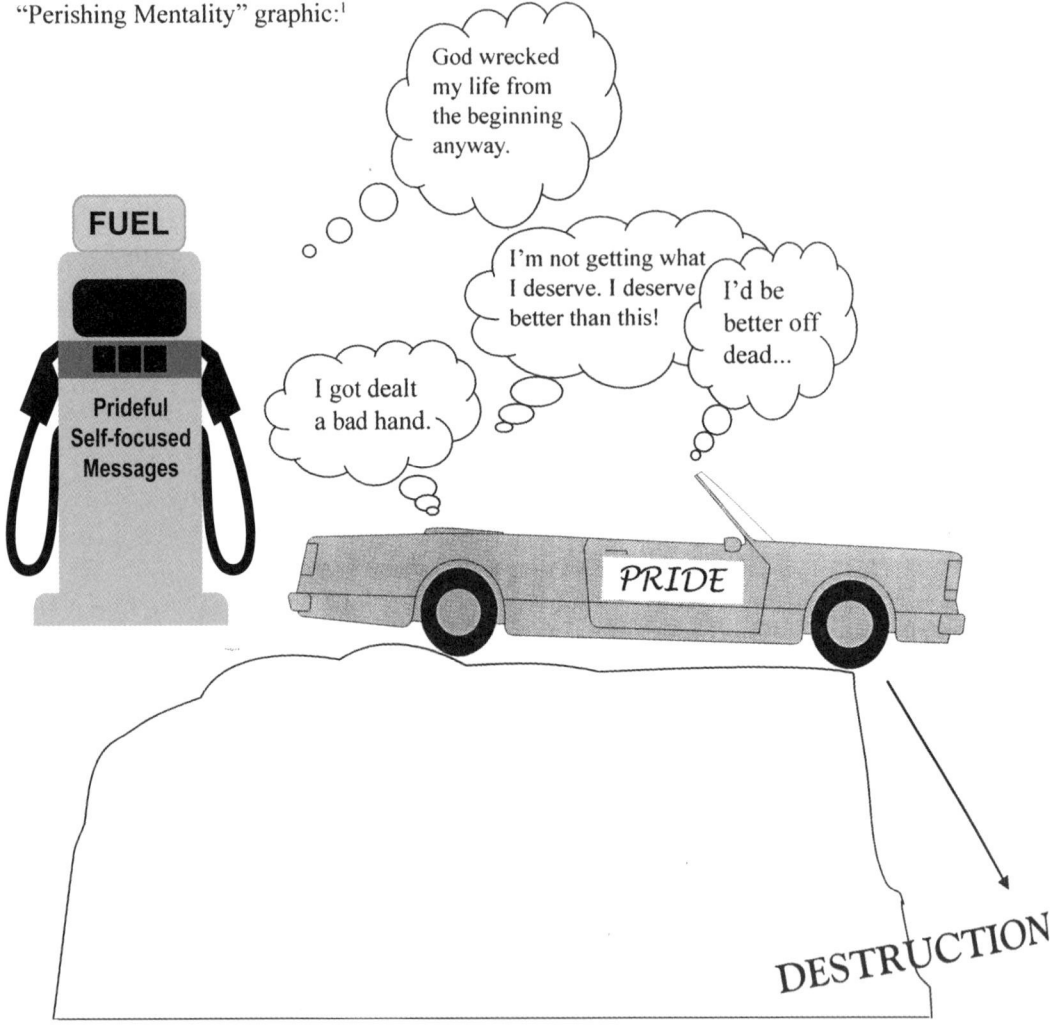

Portions of this diagram are Clipart used from ©1996 The Learning Company Inc. and its licensors.

Summary of Key Concepts from this chapter:

- ❖ *A perishing mentality often contributes to the problem of "idolatry" and substance abuse.*
- ❖ *Self-pity is thinking and focusing too much upon oneself.*
- ❖ *Thoughts are connected to emotions and actions. To bring about real change, one's ungodly thoughts must be replaced with godly thoughts.*
- ❖ *The best escape in life is to the Word of God.*

Chapter 12: Heart Problems

1. Circle the following terms that describe you:

Extremely emotional

Use extremes and superlatives in communication (like "always" or "never," "best" or "worst")

Bitter

Resentful

Supersensitive to criticism

Hurt easily

Like the "quick fix"

Avoid conflict

Find it easy to love the unlovely

Have compassion for causes like feeding the poor

Feel deeply (especially hurts)

Feel loneliness in extreme measures

Depressed often

Despair often

People-pleasing, wanting others to like me

Self-pity

Rule bender (or breaker)

Discontent

Lazy

Look for the easy way

Avoid hard work

Avoid activities that do not produce pleasure

Refuse help from others

Have an "independent" mentality of "I can do this myself"

2. Now choose at least 5 of the terms you circled above. In your journal, describe in detail how these terms that describe you are visible in your life.

3. Are you keeping any wounds fresh by playing the tape over and over in your mind of the pain? _____ Talk about this with your TCF and ask God to help you learn to grant forgiveness to those that have hurt, rejected, and offended you.

4. Answer some of the following questions about each of these hurts above:

- *How have you grown closer to the Lord as a result of this painful experience?*

_____
_____
_____

If you have not yet grown closer to the Lord, how can you begin to grow closer to Him?

_____
_____
_____

- *Create a gratitude list about the incident and the person(s) who hurt you. Practice replacing your negative, perishing thoughts about the person(s) with uplifting positive thoughts.*

_____
_____
_____

- *Write down at least 3 specific Bible verses associated with thankfulness in order to memorize them. See Appendix H in <u>The Heart of Addiction</u> text for help.*

_____
_____
_____

5. For the 5 heart problems that you circled in #1 earlier, write down the biblical alternative for those sinful attitudes:

_____
_____
_____
_____
_____

6. Contact a biblical counselor in your area today to begin working on transforming your heart attitudes. Contact www.nanc.org for help in locating a biblical counselor in your area.

Summary of Key Concepts from this chapter:
- ❖ *Do not make "feelings-oriented" decisions because you will be ruled by your flesh and its desires.*
- ❖ *Be ruled by the commands of God by learning to be "principle-oriented" from God's Word.*
- ❖ *The repentant Christian no longer has to hide, lie, or attempt to appear to be perfect because his/her identity is no longer in self, but in Christ alone.*

The Heart of Addiction Workbook

Section Two: Reproof
Chapter 13: How Many Enemies Do You Have?

1. Name the three enemies discussed in this chapter.
_____
_____
_____

2. In your opinion, rank these three enemies in order of the power they hold over you right now. Which of these seems to you to be the biggest to overcome and why?
_____
_____
_____

3. What is the difference between the Holy Spirit's conviction (John 16:8-11) and condemnation (Romans 8:1)? _____
_____

Which one applies to believers in Christ: conviction or condemnation?
_____

Which one applies to non-believers? _____

Write Romans 8:1 here: _____
_____

4. How has the world's system contributed to your sin of drunkenness?
_____
_____

5. What messages are sent via television commercials, etc.? List 3 examples of the empty promises and lies of this world?

_____
_____
_____
_____

6. List the 3 "R's" that you must do to battle in spiritual warfare.

_____
_____
_____

7. Fill in the blank: When you meditate upon Scriptural truths, it is called a "put _____."

8. When the Bible refers to your "flesh," what is it really meaning? ____

_____

9. Fill in the blank: " _____ goes before destruction and a haughty spirit before a fall." Proverbs 16:18

10. Name the three weapons you have in the struggle to confront your three Enemies:

_____
_____
_____

11. Describe in detail how you could rely upon these three weapons in your daily life.

_____
_____
_____

The Heart of Addiction Workbook

12. What hindrances might you experience in relying upon these three weapons?

_____
_____
_____

13. Write out a verse or verses of Scripture referring to one of the enemies we are studying in this chapter: _____

_____
_____

Study and memorize the verse(s).

14. Describe some situations in which reminding yourself of this Scripture might enable you to overcome the temptations set before you. _____

Summary of Key Concepts from this chapter:
- ❖ *You have three enemies. Satan and the world are external enemies. Your flesh is your internal enemy.*
- ❖ *Heart change can only occur by the power of God.*
- ❖ *The Lord has provided you with three weapons to overcome your three enemies: Jesus Christ to battle Satan; the indwelling of the Holy Spirit, and the Word of God.*

Chapter 14: The Spiritual Consequences of Addiction

1. Study Appendix D in <u>The Heart of Addiction</u> book, "More Bible Passages Related to Drunkenness" and its Consequences. Write out 3 verses to memorize in the space provided:

_____
_____
_____
_____
_____
_____
_____

2. Using your own Bible, review all the Scriptures referenced in this chapter. (You will need to refer back to the chapter in the book to look up each verse.) Write the references below:

_____
_____
_____
_____
_____

3. List the two consequences of addiction dealt with in this chapter.

_____
_____

4. List and explain how these two consequences are solved biblically.

_____
_____
_____
_____

5. Read I Thessalonians 5:19. How have you quenched the Holy Spirit's power in your life? _____
_____

How are you now seeking to enable the Holy Spirit to flow through you and to change your thinking? _____

Summary of Key Concepts from this chapter:
- ❖ *You can quench the Holy Spirit, but humility, brokenness, and submission will enable you to be led by the Holy Spirit again.*
- ❖ *You can sear your conscience by continually sinning but repentance is the way to find the mercy of God and to begin listening to Him again.*
- ❖ *Listening to God is accomplished by reading and studying the Word of God.*

Chapter 15: Manifestations of Pride

1. Name the 3 ways that pride is commonly manifested.

2. How is self-pity related to pride?

3. In what three ways was Jesus tempted?

4. In what specific way did Jesus respond to each of the three temptations?

5. How are these temptations manifested in your life?

6. In what specific ways can you respond to these temptations in your life?

7. What is the opposite (or antidote) for pride?
_____
_____

8. List 3 ways you can begin to be "meek" and "humble" in your everyday life.
_____
_____
_____

Summary of Key Concepts from this chapter:
- ❖ *The lust of the flesh, lust of the eyes, and the pride of life are basic temptations for all of us.*
- ❖ *Adam and Eve fell to these temptations by choosing to sin against God resulting in the consequent curses and death spoken by God in Genesis 3: upon the serpent, upon Satan, upon the woman, the man, and the earth itself.*
- ❖ *Though tempted in the same manner as Adam, Jesus overcame the temptation by choosing not to sin AND choosing to rightly apply God's Word to His situation. Knowing the truth of God's Word is of vital importance for us when battling the lies of Satan.*

Chapter 16: What to do First: Put-Off

1. List and describe 3-5 specific ways God has called you to humility by allowing consequences and/or circumstances resulting from your sin of drunken and/or addictive behavior.

_____
_____
_____
_____
_____

2. Are you facing the "Insurmountable Wall"? _____ Ask your TCF to evaluate whether or not he/she believes you are facing the "Insurmountable Wall" of not accepting full responsibility for your sinful actions of the past and present. Remember that the path to freedom in Christ, the path of transformation, and the path to eternal life is straight and narrow and there are few that find it.

3. Is denial, or self-deception, still prohibiting you from experiencing the gift of forgiveness from God and others?_____

Have you fully accepted responsibility for your sins or are you trying to climb the "insurmountable wall" of denial, self-deception, and blame-shifting? _____

In what ways have you practically and verbally accepted responsibility? _____
_____

4. Review every Scripture mentioned in this chapter. Write your favorite one down on a 3" x 5" card or piece of paper and meditate upon it daily for one week.

6. Ask yourself: Am I faithful in my assignments or am I half-heartedly applying myself to this study? ____ Ask your TCF to evaluate your faithfulness on a scale of 1 to 10 (10 being the best). Put his/her numerical assessment here: _____

7. Use Appendix F in <u>The Heart of Addiction</u> to set up restrictions, or boundaries, so that you may depend upon God and others to help you overcome your addiction. Discuss your work on Appendix F with your TCF.

8. If you are failing miserably in your attempt to live with the responsibility and submission that is described in this chapter, pray the prayer listed at the end of the chapter:

God, My Father, I have looked for short cuts and the easy way out. The familiar road of my sinful habits of drunkenness have been more appealing to me than taking responsibility and submitting to others and ultimately to You, Dear Lord. Save me from this wretched trap. Help me turn from my way, trusting in You, Lord Jesus Christ, alone for my salvation. Help me trust in the work of your Holy Spirit and submit to and apply the biblical principles and practical wisdom You are teaching me. Amen.

Summary of Key Concepts from this chapter:
- ***Putting-off sin is the first part of battling idolatry, drunkenness, and "addiction."***
- ***You may be deceiving yourself through an unwillingness to be teachable and open to God's truth.***
- ***Ask the Lord to make you willing to hear and obey His Word and recognize that His commands are good.***

Section Three: Correction
Chapter 17: What to Do Second: Renewing Your Mind

1. Refer back to your list of Put-off's from Appendix C in <u>The Heart of Addiction</u>. Now, look at the following thoughts you may have had since we began this journey on the path of transformation from the beginning of the book. Below each item on the list, write a biblical truth to counteract (oppose) the lie that is being suggested. List the specific Bible verse if you can.

a) "This is too hard! Just give up." _____

b) "It's really not my fault." _____

c) "I am lost – there's no hope." _____

d) "How can God forgive me for that?" _____

e) "My sins are too big to overcome." _____

f) "It will always be there in my mind. I can't stop my thoughts from happening."
_____

2. Explain why referring to your actions as "drunkenness" gives you more hope.
_____
_____

Discuss this answer with your TCF.

3. What is the primary goal of biblical counseling? _____
_____
_____

4. Find a Scripture passage that supports why this should be your goal.
_____
_____

5. Is it a sin for YOU to drink alcohol or use drugs in an abusive manner at this point in your life? _____

Does the term drunkenness accurately describe your sin? _____

6. Did you make the connection between the Holy Spirit and the Bible in the process of transformation? _____

Explain the connection between the Holy Spirit and Bible in your own words: ____
_____
_____

7. According to Ephesians 5:18, is it a sin to be drunk with wine to excess?
_____

8. Does God ever ask our opinion about His commands in the Bible?
_____

9. What are the attitudes listed as chapter sub-headings that one must possess in order to be "set right" with God?
A Teachable _____
A Learner's _____
A Practitioner's _____

What do each of these mean in your own words based upon your reading? _____
_____
_____

10. In your own words, how important is your mind in the battle of drunkenness and idolatry? _____
_____

Summary of Key Concepts from this chapter:

- ❖ *A teachable spirit is important because God knows better than any person, including you.*
- ❖ *A learner's heart is important because you need to know what God says about defeating your enemies.*
- ❖ *A practitioner's commitment is important because we are commanded to be doers of God's Word and not just hearers of it. All three of these attitudes require humility.*

Chapter 18: The Battle in the Mind

1. What is the most powerful weapon against cravings? _____
(Hint: Knowing the _____ of _____)

2. What does it mean to "take a thought captive" according to 2 Corinthians 10:5? _____

3. What do you replace that "captive thought" (or lie) with? _____

4. List the seven practical ways to resist the devil and the temptations to sin:

1) _____

2) _____

3) _____

4) _____

5) _____

6) _____

7) _____

5. Proverbs 27:6 states: "Faithful are the wounds of a friend; profuse are the kisses of an enemy." Do you have real friends now who may wound you but for your ultimate good? _____

Who are those friends? _____

If you do not have those friends, who can you ask to be a real, authentic, and truth-telling friend to you? _____

6. What does being godly look like? Use the scale of 1–10 to rate yourself in how you display the fruit of the Spirit in your life (Galatians 5:22-23).

Love
1   2   3   4   5   6   7   8   9   10

Joy
1   2   3   4   5   6   7   8   9   10

Peace
1   2   3   4   5   6   7   8   9   10

Patience
1   2   3   4   5   6   7   8   9   10

Kindness
1   2   3   4   5   6   7   8   9   10

Goodness
1   2   3   4   5   6   7   8   9   10

Faithfulness
1   2   3   4   5   6   7   8   9   10

Gentleness
1   2   3   4   5   6   7   8   9   10

Self-Control
1   2   3   4   5   6   7   8   9   10

7. Ask your TCF to use the scale of 1–10 to rate you in the displaying of the fruit of the Spirit in your life (Galatians 5:22-23).

Love
1   2   3   4   5   6   7   8   9   10

Joy
1   2   3   4   5   6   7   8   9   10

Peace
1   2   3   4   5   6   7   8   9   10

Patience
1   2   3   4   5   6   7   8   9   10

Kindness

1   2   3   4   5   6   7   8   9   10

Goodness

1   2   3   4   5   6   7   8   9   10

Faithfulness

1   2   3   4   5   6   7   8   9   10

Gentleness

1   2   3   4   5   6   7   8   9   10

Self-Control

1   2   3   4   5   6   7   8   9   10

Summary of Key Concepts from this chapter:
- ❖ *Renewing your mind is essential in overcoming any "addiction."*
- ❖ *Fighting physical cravings begins in your mind.*
- ❖ *Thoughts must be taken captive when they are unbiblical and ungodly. Then those thoughts must be replaced by biblical and godly ones founded in Christ and the Word of God.*

Section Four: Training in Righteousness
Chapter 19: What to Do Third: Put-on

1. What people, places, and things have you been able to put off since the beginning of your study? (Refer to Appendix C in <u>The Heart of Addiction</u>)

_____
_____

2. Have you put-off the victim mentality? _____

Have you put off blaming demons, parents, others, and your experiences in the past? _____

Have you put off the labeling and minimizing of your sin with worldly terminology? _____

If so, what are you now putting-on to replace each of the above questions? _____
_____

3. Name some things you have already put on as a result of having started the study in this book.

_____
_____
_____

4. Have you put on acknowledgement of your sin? _____

Have you put on listening to others? _____

Have you put on attendance at church? _____

Have you put on a new definition of your problem? _____

Have you put on reading and studying the Bible? _____

Have you put on expressing your heart to God your Father? _____

Have you put on new relationships with godly mature Christian believers who care about you? _____

5. How are you now specifically renewing your mind? Name three specific things you are now doing to renew your mind. These are things that you were not doing in your previous attempts at overcoming the sins of drunkenness.

_____
_____
_____
_____
_____
_____

6. Discuss with your TCF how repentance is part of the daily Christian walk as opposed to a one-time experience. _____
_____
_____

7. Fill in the blank: "Wisdom is both hearing and _____ what is right in a way that pleases God first."

Summary of Key Concepts from this chapter:
- ❖ *Wisdom is not just knowing facts, but putting them into practice. Wisdom is being a doer of the Word and not just a hearer only.*
- ❖ *Consequences often produce humility which should bring you to the foot of the cross of Jesus Christ.*
- ❖ *Repentance must become part of your daily walk with God and with others. Get in the habit of asking for the forgiveness of others.*

Chapter 20: Responsibility, Gratitude, and Submission: More to Put On

1. In your journal, describe one or two occasions in which you have experienced godly sorrow.

2. In your journal, describe two other examples of worldly sorrow you may have experienced.

3. Describe some concrete and practical ways in which you could demonstrate responsibility in your life now.

_____
_____
_____

Discuss with your TCF the potential difficulties you may encounter as you try to implement this plan and prepare in advance what you will do to be successful.

4. What is the difference between confession and admission? _____

_____
_____

5. In your journal, describe two situations in which you confessed vs. admitted your guilt regarding some past incident.

6. Memorize I John 1:9-10. Write it on a 3"x 5" card or small piece of paper and carry it in your pocket or purse to meditate upon throughout the day.

7. What mentality replaces the perishing mentality?

_____

8. What is the "good" in Romans 8:28 that benefits the transformed addict?

_____

9. In what specific ways have you not been submissive or teachable in your past efforts to change? _____

_____

How will it be different this time?

_____
_____
_____

10. What warning is given in the book regarding group meetings? _____

_____
_____

Have you experienced the pros and cons of self-help group meetings? List the pros and cons you've experienced below:

PROS _____
_____
_____

CONS _____
_____
_____
_____
_____

Note: Small groups led by a TCF are fine as long as they seek to honor Christ and not gossip or glorify sin.

Responsibility, Gratitude and Submission

11. Find a group of the same gender to join in order to study the Bible, pray, and honestly discuss the challenges of the Christian walk. Ask your TCF to lead it or to help you find one.

12. If you have not done so already, complete Appendix F to help you schedule your days, weeks, and months.

13. List all of "God's Mighty Resources for You."

_____
_____
_____
_____
_____

14. Is there evidence that you are becoming more responsible in your daily life? _____ **An example of increased responsibility is "being where you say you are going to be when you say you will be there." In other words, being responsible occurs when your words match your deeds. List the recent examples and evidence in your life that demonstrate you are being more responsible.** (You may have to ask your TCF for help.)

_____
_____
_____
_____
_____

15. Is there evidence that you are becoming more grateful in your daily life? _____ **Are you replacing a "perishing mentality" with thankfulness and joy? List the recent evidence in your life.** (You may have to ask your TCF for help.)

_____
_____
_____
_____
_____

The Heart of Addiction Workbook

16. Is there evidence that you are becoming more submissive to authorities in your daily life? List the evidence. (You may have to ask your TCF for help.)

_____
_____
_____
_____
_____
_____

17. What does "submission" mean? _____

Are you willing to do what your authorities ask of you? _____

Ask your TCF how you can be more trusting of Christ and submissive to the authorities in your life? _____

Summary of Key Concepts from this chapter:
- ❖ *Responsibility is a put-on and a key ingredient in the growth of an "addict" and idolater. Confession of sins is essential as Jesus died for our sins.*
- ❖ *Gratitude is a new, heavenly mindset that replaces the perishing mentality.*
- ❖ *Submission is the willing placement of yourself underneath someone else's authority which demonstrates that you do not demand to be "in charge" of your own life any longer, but rather are trusting Christ and those He has placed in authority over you.*

Chapter 21: Seven Things for Which to Pray

1. For the next seven days, re-read each section in Chapter 21 of <u>The Heart of Addiction</u> book (one section per day). Pray each day that God will grant to you that prayer request according to His Will and Perfect Plan.

DAY 1

DAY 2

DAY 3

DAY 4

DAY 5

DAY 6

DAY 7

2. Ask your prayer partner specifically to pray with you for these seven things. Write some of your thoughts out to God in your journal.

3. Obtain a copy of the pamphlet entitled "7 Minutes With God: How to Plan a Daily Quiet Time"[7] and discuss it with your TCF.

4. If you have not done so already, write out your life story. Use Appendix J in <u>The Heart of Addiction</u> book to help you. Write it in your journal/notebook.

5. Pray for each of the following 7 persons each day during the upcoming week:

a) pastor

b) physician

c) prayer partner

---

[7] Foster, Robert D., "Seven Minutes with God," Navpress, Colorado Springs, CO.

d) TCF

e) Church leader of choice

f) biblical counselor

g) someone else of your choice (write name here): _____

Summary of Key Concepts from this chapter:
- ❖ *Prayer is essential and is the primary work of the Christian.*
- ❖ *Ask God to give you a passion for biblical prayer.*
- ❖ *Pray utilizing the principles from God's Word so that you develop a mind like Christ's.*

Chapter 22: Taking a Nazirite Vow Under the Care of a Physician

1. Review your put off and put on lists from Appendix C so you can use it to complete #2 below.

2. Pray about developing a plan to submit yourself to the care of a physician for the purpose of glorifying God in the area of substance abuse.

3. Write out a detailed plan, in your journal, to implement the ideas of this chapter in your life. Consider all aspects of this plan including your employment situation, your family responsibilities, and your legal issues, if any. Be specific.

4. Discuss your plans regarding your implementation of this chapter with your:

a) pastor

b) physician

c) prayer partner

d) TCF

e) Church leader of choice

f) biblical counselor

5. Submit yourself to your leaders' counsel as long as it is biblically grounded.

Summary of Key Concepts from this chapter:
- ❖ *Develop a relationship with a primary care physician.*
- ❖ *Prayerfully consider taking a Nazirite vow willingly unto the Lord for the next six months.*
- ❖ *Ask the Lord to clear your head and physical body during those six months so that you may obey Him and hear Him better.*

Chapter 23: Controlled by the Holy Spirit

1. Much has been misunderstood about the person of the Holy Spirit. The Holy Spirit is a not an "It." He is a Person of the Trinity.

The Holy Spirit is sent by the Father – after the atoning work of the Son was completed at Calvary – to those believers who are living by faith in the Son of God alone for their salvation. The Holy Spirit leads the transforming Christian addict primarily by, and through, the Word of God. Here is the most exciting thing about the presence of the Holy Spirit in your life: "When you put more of the Word of God in your mind, the Holy Spirit will have more to work with to empower you in your thoughts, feelings, and actions." In other words, as you study the Bible faithfully, you will gain wisdom and power so that you can obey God and experience blessings! Write down your understanding of this concept in your own words.

_____
_____
_____

2. Discuss your understanding of the Holy Spirit's work in your life with your TCF.

3. Write down your previous views of the word "self-control."

_____
_____

4. Write down your new understanding of what it means to have "self" be the object of control by the Holy Spirit in your life.

_____
_____

5. Discuss with your TCF how this new view of self-control will enable you to be more victorious in your struggle with sin.

6. Describe what is meant by the term "sanctification" and how it is a process:

_____
_____
_____

7. Do you find yourself despising the concepts of submission, self-control, and discipline? _____

Write down 5 verses/passages of Scripture related to these concepts.

_____
_____
_____
_____
_____

Discuss it with your TCF.

8. Read I Corinthians 9:24-27. How have you begun to be careful with your body (what goes in it, what you see, where you go, how much sleep you get) now that you are beginning to realize the battle you are in with your flesh? Use your journal if you need more room to write.

_____
_____
_____

If you have not begun this battle, ask God to forgive you for waiting this long to start resisting. Pray for the strength to resist your enemies, and begin to exercise self-control in all things.

9. Read I Timothy 4:7-8 aloud. Describe the importance of beginning now to discipline your body for godliness.

_____
_____
_____

10. If you should fail again and "relapse," then what do you know happened?

_____
_____

The answer to the above question is that you were <u>not walking in the Holy Spirit</u> but were <u>walking in the desires and appetites of your flesh</u>. You gave into your feelings and lusts of your flesh. It was very likely a sinful choice.

Therefore, what should you do <u>if</u> you fail and sin by using drugs and/or alcohol again? _____
_____

The answer to the above question is to <u>repent</u> and <u>believe in the Lord Jesus Christ</u>. In other words, confess your sin to God in prayer, ask Him to forgive you based upon the atoning blood sacrifice of Jesus Christ, and then trust in Him again to use this temporary defeat for good in your life. God will also provide strength for you in the battle against any "addiction" or idolatrous desire.

11. Read Romans 5:20-21. Through Jesus Christ, God's grace is mightier than any and all of our sins!

Summary of Key Concepts from this chapter:
- ❖ *Understand that your "self" is not the source of control.*
- ❖ *Understand that your "self" is the object being controlled.*
- ❖ *Understand that the Holy Spirit is the source of control for your "self."*

Chapter 24: Focus Upon Others

1. Make a list of 20 people that you can encourage and/or bless by a phone call, an email, a letter, a smile, or a kind word today. By each person's name, put how you would encourage them. Put a check mark by each after you contact them!

_____   _____
_____   _____
_____   _____
_____   _____
_____   _____
_____   _____
_____   _____
_____   _____
_____   _____
_____   _____
_____   _____
_____   _____
_____   _____
_____   _____
_____   _____
_____   _____
_____   _____
_____   _____
_____   _____
_____   _____

2. Contact one of the above persons each day for the next 20 days in at least one way.

3. Make a list of recently selfish acts. Next to each listed selfish act, make a list of selfless acts that you could do instead. Make this a realistic list, not a list of things that you would never be able to accomplish in a day. If you desire, you may make a long-term list as well.

Here is an example:

Watched TV 4 hours _____   Spent time with spouse/children _____

_____   _____
_____   _____
_____   _____
_____   _____
_____   _____
_____   _____
_____   _____
_____   _____

4. Make daily entries in your journal for two weeks about ways in which you have received instruction, admonition, counsel, encouragement, and blessing from someone else.

5. Now, take that list of instruction, admonition, counsel, encouragement, and blessing and do them for someone else that you know.

For example:

Teach someone today about one of the things that you learned.

Encourage someone today with the same encouragement you received.

Listen to someone else's problems and pray for them.

Tell them that you have prayed for them.

Send them an encouraging letter that explains how you have prayed for them.

(Pick at least 2 of the above to put into action toward someone else.)

6. In your journal, write briefly about your experiences, feelings, and thoughts about how you helped someone today.

7. Go back and read something that you wrote in your journal and share it with someone. Tell them how God has shown you new things and has changed you since then.

8. Write an entry in your journal addressed to yourself to be read a year from now. Encourage yourself to remember the most important things you have learned from this study and summarize them in a page or two.

9. What are two new, biblical slogans for your life?
_____
_____

10. Read II Corinthians 1:3-5. Write about how you can apply these verses by telling others who struggle with addictions about the sufferings you have experienced.
_____
_____
_____
_____
_____
_____

Summary of Key Concepts from this chapter:
- ❖ *Focus upon how you can serve the Lord by serving others.*
- ❖ *It is more blessed to give than to receive.*
- ❖ *Be careful not to offend others in your walk with Christ.*

Chapter 25: The End of the Matter is Just the Beginning

1. Review. Write out the definition of the following terms.

a) Abuse: _____

b) Addiction as redefined earlier: _____

c) Perishing mentality: _____

2. List six ways to create godly habits of worship in your daily life.

_____
_____
_____
_____
_____
_____

3. Summarize what this book is about in three main points.

_____
_____
_____

4. What are three things that you can share with others that would encourage them as a result of this intensive Bible study?

_____
_____
_____

5. What do you most look forward to in your new life in Christ without the bondage of alcohol and drugs?

_____
_____
_____

Summary of Key Concepts from this chapter:

- ❖ *Knowing the Lord personally and intimately is a primary desire of all our hearts.*
- ❖ *God is love and He is good. God can be trusted with your problem of "addiction." His grace is sufficient for you!*
- ❖ *Rather than fulfilling selfish, fleshly desires, loving and serving God are the only ways for mankind to find true fulfillment and purpose in this life. This is simply called "worshiping God" (I Corinthians 10:31).*

Additional Bible Study on "Drunkenness"

For deeper study, turn to Appendix D in The Heart of Addiction book. There are 27 passages of Scripture listed at the bottom of that Appendix. Use this list to go deeper by doing the following:

1. Read each passage listed in Appendix D separately and then complete the questions below for each passage.

2. Write your answers to the following questions in your journal/ notebook:

a) What are the facts related to drunkenness in this passage?

b) What consequences did (or will) occur from this passage?

c) What life lesson can I apply to my situation?

d) In what way is my loving Father protecting me by commanding me to refrain from drunkenness based upon this passage?